I0116464

Lorikeet's Welcome Colin Cockatoo
Second Edition

Rainbow Lorikeets are so full of life, their fun-loving, mischievous nature is captivating.

This story, the fourth in the Lorikeet's Book Series for young readers, is based on a family of Lorikeets who have a visit from a very nervous Sulphur Crested Cockatoo.

Through my words and the creative vision of Lillian Falzon, whose illustrations brought these characters to life, I hope you enjoy a peek into the adventures of this quirky, colourful family.

It's a very hot day, the grass is dry and brittle. The sky is blue with a few fluffy white clouds skipping by overhead, a gentle breeze dances through the leaves at the top of the trees.

Seeds, blossoms and nuts, the usual diet for Lorikeets and Parrots, are scarce this time of year.

Lawrence the Rainbow Lorikeet wants to ensure his family are fed and remembers there are sunflower seeds in a nearby garden they had visited before.

Lawrence calls his family and before long, Loretta and the chicks are flying with Lawrence to the garden, darting around, screeching and chattering under the shade of the treed canopy.

In the garden, there is a stranger in one of the trees above watching the Lorikeets singing and flying from feeder to feeder, enjoying the late afternoon treats.

The chicks point out the stranger to their father
Lawrence and ask if they are safe.

Lawrence ensures the chicks that no harm will come
to them as the stranger in the tree above the garden is
Colin the Cockatoo, a distant relative.

Colin the Sulphur Crested Cockatoo looks spectacular
with his shiny black eyes and hooked beak.

His yellow plume, brilliant white jacket, bloomers and
vest are stunning.

Colin the Cockatoo has no mate and is alone in the
tree.

Colin watches the family of Lorikeets closely for the longest time, he isn't as comfortable as the Lorikeet family to fly down from the safety of the trees to the trays.

Colin decides to take a closer look. He flies to a tree nearer to the trays and sees there are seeds in the trays.

Colin looks around to see the Lorikeets are not interested in what he is doing and are busily eating and playing whilst he nervously scans the area for danger.

Finally, Colin flies to a tray, he lands awkwardly as his big claws struggle to grip the edge to balance his large body.

Still not sure of his surroundings, he looks about the garden, picks up a sunflower seed in his large black beak and splits open the husk to enjoy the juicy centre.

Again Colin looks around the garden, he picks up another seed in his beak, splits it open and enjoys the seed.

This process of looking around picking up a seed, splitting and eating goes on for quite a while. Suddenly Colin is spooked and flies up high into the trees.

Colin sees the Lorikeet family did not fly off. He decides there is no danger and flies down from the tree, returning to the tray, this time clinging to the edge tightly and quickly gaining his balance.

Colin resumes eating as per his ritual of looking around, picking up a seed, splitting and enjoying the juicy centre.

Lawrence and Loretta's chicks Laura, Lance, Leroy and Lana decide to welcome Colin and fly over to join Colin on his tray.

Colin is not sure about these noisy chicks and stands tall, the stunning yellow plume on his head separates like a fan, he stretches out his very large white wings, which are yellow underneath and holds on tight.

The chicks are surprised by this sudden display and fly to the ground and happily retrieve the seeds that have been dropped, leaving the tray to Colin.

The hot red sun is beginning to go down behind the hill. Lawrence screeches, summoning his family.

The Rainbow Lorikeet family take flight, the red lining of their brightly coloured green coats makes a beautiful display as they fly away into the distance, chatting and chirping.

Colin the Cockatoo is alone in the garden and soon
misses his new-found friends.

He has a few more seeds and then flies away swaarking,
knowing he has somewhere to visit again where he won't
be alone.

Lorikeet's Welcome Colin Cockatoo

ISBN

978-1-7640295-7-5 (Paperback)

978-1-7640295-8-2 (eBook)

www.ingramcontent.com/pod-product-compliance
Lightning Source LLC
Chambersburg PA
CBHW060842270326
41933CB00002B/170